Linking art to the world around us

Arty Facts

Oceans
& Art Activities

Crabtree Publishing Company
www.crabtreebooks.com

Crabtree Publishing Company

PMB 16A, 350 Fifth Avenue, Suite 3308
New York, NY
10118

612 Welland Avenue
St. Catharines, Ontario
L2M 5V6

Coordinating Editor: Ellen Rodger
Project Editors: P.A. Finlay, Carrie Gleason
Production Coordinator: Rosie Gowsell

Project Development and Concept Marshall Direct:
Editorial Project Director: Karen Foster
Editors: Claire Sippi, Hazel Songhurst, Samantha Sweeney
Researchers: Gerry Bailey, Alec Edgington
Design Director: Tracy Carrington
Designers: Claire Penny, Paul Montague,
James Thompson, Mark Dempsey
Production: Victoria Grimsell, Christina Brown
Photo Research: Andrea Sadler
Illustrator: Jan Smith
Model Artist: Sophie Dean

Prepress, printing, and binding by Worzalla Publishing Company

Sacks, Janet.
   Oceans and art activities / written by Janet Sacks and Polly Goodman.
      p. cm. -- (Arty facts)
Includes index.
   Summary: Information about various topics related to the plants, animals, impact of
humans, and composition of oceans forms the foundation for a variety of craft projects.
   ISBN 0-7787-1143-9 (rlb) -- ISBN 0-7787-1115-3 (pbk)
   1. Marine ecology--Juvenile literature. 2. Ocean--Juvenile literature. 3. Marine
ecology--Study and teaching (Elementary)--Activity programs. 4. Ocean--Study and
teaching (Elementary)--Activity programs [1. Marine ecology. 2. Ecology. 3. Ocean. 4.
Handicraft.] I. Goodman, Polly. II. Title. III. Series.
   QH541.5.S3 S227 2003
   551.46--dc21
                                                        2002011631
                                                            LC

Created by
Marshall Direct Learning

© 2002 Marshall Direct Learning

FRONT COVER IMAGES: C & S HOOD/ BRUCE COLEMAN COLLECTION; MALCOLM HEY/ BRUCE COLEMAN COLLECTION; JEFF FOOTT/ BBC NATURAL HISTORY UNIT/ PACIFIC STOCK/ BRUCE COLEMAN COLLECTION

Linking art to the world around us

Arty Facts

Oceans
& Art Activities

Contents

WRITTEN BY Janet Sacks and Polly Goodman

Deep blue sea

When we think of the sea or ocean, we usually picture large areas of blue-green water. The color of the water in the sea depends on the light that shines on it. It also depends on how the light is reflected and **absorbed** by the water.

Blue sea

When light enters the sea, the water reflects some of it and absorbs some of it. Daylight is a mixture of many different colors of light, and these colors are reflected and absorbed in different amounts. Water hardly absorbs any blue-green light, but reflects it more than any other color of light. This reflection of the blue-green light off the water is what makes the sea appear blue or green.

Deep sea

The deeper we go in the sea, the more light is absorbed. Below 3,280 feet (1,000 m), the water of the ocean is almost completely dark. Here, some marine animals have body parts that produce light. Other animals have light-making **bacteria** that live in their body.

Salty water

Seawater is not pure water. It contains chemical elements found in rocks, which have dissolved over a long period. **Chlorine**, sodium, sulphur, magnesium, **calcium,** and potassium are the most common elements in seawater. The **salt** in the sea is sodium chloride, which is the same as table salt. The amount of salt in the sea can vary. The water is **denser** and the color is darker where there is a lot of salt.

Oceans

Underwater picture

Fill your sea scene with shades of color

WHAT YOU NEED

poster board

paper

pencil

scissors

pencil crayons

tissue paper

glue

wire

1 Use the pencil crayons to draw and color shapes of fish, shells, starfish, rocks, and seaweed on paper. Cut out the shapes.

2 Glue the shapes onto the poster board.

3 Tear pieces of tissue paper and glue them onto the poster board, overlapping the shapes to create different shades of color.

4 Wrap tissue paper around a piece of wire to make seaweed, and glue it onto your picture.

Overlap the shapes for a **3-D** effect

5

Seaweed power

Y ou have probably seen seaweed on a beach, lying on the sand or clinging to pebbles on the shore. Seaweed is an important part of ocean and shore life, because it offers shelter and is a nutritious food for some sea animals.

What is seaweed?

All seaweed are simple plants called algae, which do not have roots, stems, leaves, or flowers like other plants. Seaweed is full of **nutrients**, and is an important source of food for animals that live on the shore, such as mussels and crabs. Seaweed can be green, brown, red, or even purple. Seaweed does not grow deeper than 656 feet (200 m) below the water's surface because it needs sunlight to survive. Large seaweed, such as **kelp**, have root-like parts that anchor them to rocks or to the seabed. Smaller seaweed, such as bladder wrack, have air-filled bubbles on their **fronds** that enable them to float.

Kelp forests

There are thousands of different species of seaweed. Seaweed plants range in size from as small as the tip of a pencil to 328 feet (100 m) long. Giant kelp grows faster than any other plant – up to 12 inches (30 cm) a day. With its hundreds of branches, kelp provides food and shelter for many underwater animals.

Oceans

Seaweed collage

1 Draw outlines of different shapes of seaweed on paper. Paint and decorate with sequins.

2 Let the seaweed or grass you have collected dry out. Glue it on top of your painting.

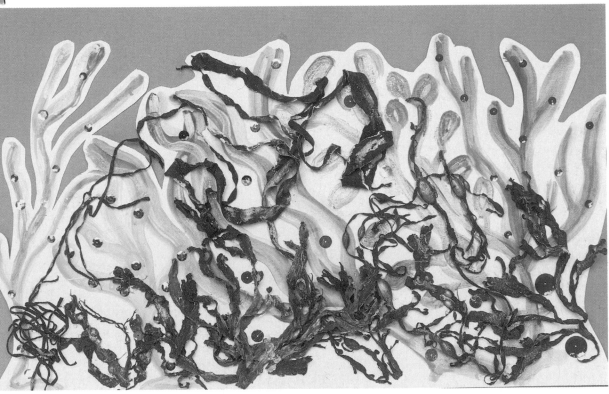

What other pictures can you make with your seaweed?

3 Cut around the seaweed outlines and mount the picture on poster board.

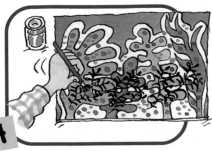

4 Add specks of gold paint to your seaweed picture.

Jellyfish

Jellyfish drift in the ocean, trailing long **tentacles** beneath their umbrella-shaped bodies. These jelly-like bodies can be tinted red, brown, blue, yellow, or mauve according to the color of the water or what they eat. The jellyfish's almost see-through body helps **camouflage** it in the open ocean, where there is nowhere to hide.

What are jellyfish?

Jellyfish have been around for more than 650 million years, even before dinosaurs roamed the Earth! They are not a type of fish, but belong to the invertebrate family, which means they do not have a backbone. Ninety-five percent of a jellyfish's body is made up of water. A jellyfish does not have a heart, a brain, or eyes – just a jelly-like body and tentacles to catch and stun food. The lion's mane jellyfish is the largest jellyfish, with an 8 foot (2.4 m) body and tentacles longer than half a soccer field.

Water acrobats

Jellyfish drift with the ocean's **current**, but they can also swim using **jet propulsion**. Water is pushed out of its body, making the jellyfish move forward.

A powerful sting

Jellyfish use their stinging tentacles to catch food and protect themselves. When they sense another animal's movements, the jellyfish's stinging **cells** shoot tiny tubes containing poison into the **prey**. The poison stuns or kills the prey.

A beautiful lagoon jellyfish.

Oceans

Tickly tentacles

WHAT YOU NEED

newspaper

balloon

glue

ribbon

tin foil   sequins

glitter

bubble wrap

paints and brush

thread

scissors

cellophane

1

Blow up a balloon. Tear pieces of newspaper and glue them over the top half of the balloon. When dry, pop the balloon.

2 Paint and decorate the jellyfish body with glitter, sequins, foil, and pieces of bubble wrap.

3 Twist pieces of cellophane and foil, and glue to the inside of the jellyfish's body.

4

Cut smaller pieces of ribbon and glue to the inside.

Attach a piece of thread from the center of the body so you can hang your jellyfish from the ceiling.

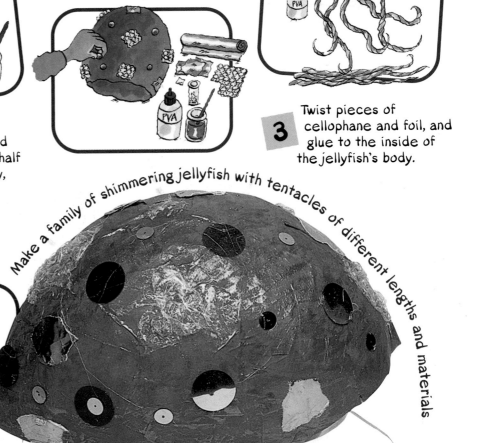

Make a family of shimmering jellyfish with tentacles of different lengths and materials

Claws and pincers

On the beach, you may see a prawn paddling in a tidal pool or a crab burying itself in the sand. These animals, as well as lobsters, shrimp, **krill**, barnacles, and crayfish, belong to the family of **crustaceans**. These sea animals have a tough outer shell and many jointed legs.

Crabs

Hundreds of different types of crabs live on shores in different parts of the world. Crabs have a shell, four pairs of legs, with which they walk sideways, and two claws for holding their prey. The hermit crab does not have its own shell, but carries the empty shells of snails or other **mollusks**.

Big and small

The biggest crab is the giant spider crab, whose outstretched claws can measure more than 13 feet (4 m), or long enough to hug a hippopotamus! Spider crabs differ from other crabs because they cover themselves with living **sponge** and seaweed and let these grow on them as a disguise. The smallest crab is the pea crab, which lives inside the shells of oysters and mussels. The male fiddler crab has one large claw, which he uses to threaten other males and attract a female, and a smaller claw he uses for eating.

Prawns and shrimp

Can you tell the difference between a shrimp and a prawn? A prawn has delicate claws on its front legs and a saw-like horn on its head. A shrimp's front legs are broad and flat and it has no horn. **Tropical** prawns grow as large as small lobsters. Some prawns and shrimps change color to match their surroundings.

Lobsters

Common lobsters come out of their rocky hiding places at night to look for food. Their two great claws crush, hold, and tear their prey. Lobsters can re-grow their claws if they lose them in a fight!

A fiddler crab.

Oceans

WHAT YOU NEED

paints and brush

elastic

tin foil

glue

sequins

two jar lids

shells

scissors

sponge

Clicking castanets

1 Cover two jar lids with tin foil.

2 Ask an adult to help you make holes in one edge of each lid with the scissors. Thread a piece of elastic through the holes and tie the ends together.

Make other castanets for your friends so you can all click together!

3 Cut pieces of sponge, and glue them onto the tops of the lids. Paint the sponges.

4 Glue shells and sequins onto the sponges. Your castanets are now ready for clicking!

Fishing nets

Traditional fishing

People have fished in different ways for thousands of years without **endangering** fish populations. Some people fish by throwing **harpoons**, others set traps, and many people fish off coastal villages using small boats.

Freezing the catch

In the modern fishing industry, large refrigerator ships stay at sea for months at a time. The fish is frozen on the boat so that it does not rot before it gets to the supermarkets.

Animals in danger

Nets are used to catch a large number of fish at one time. Drift nets are sometimes 30 feet (9 m) long. These nets float behind boats to catch fish that swim at the surface, such as herring, salmon, and tuna. Other marine animals, such as turtles, seals, and sea birds, are killed when they get caught in the nets. Purse nets scoop up large shoals, or schools, of tuna, but dolphins also get swept up in the nets. Purse nets are now banned in countries around the world to protect the dolphins. Boats that drag large nets along the seabed are called trawlers. When these boats trawl, or skim the seabed for sole and rays, large numbers of worms and shellfish, which fish feed on, are also killed in the nets. Every year, countries agree on the maximum number of fish that they will catch. This helps the situation, but overfishing is still a problem.

People all over the world eat fish. Each year about 77 tons (70 tonnes) of fish, especially sardines, Atlantic cod, and mackerel, are caught in the oceans. Today, people are **overfishing**, and the fish caught are younger and smaller. Fishers are not waiting long enough for the fish to grow before catching them.

Oceans

Hook-a-fish game

WHAT YOU NEED

styrofoam

tissue paper

sequins

wire

straws

scissors

poster board

silver foil

paints and brush

glue

string

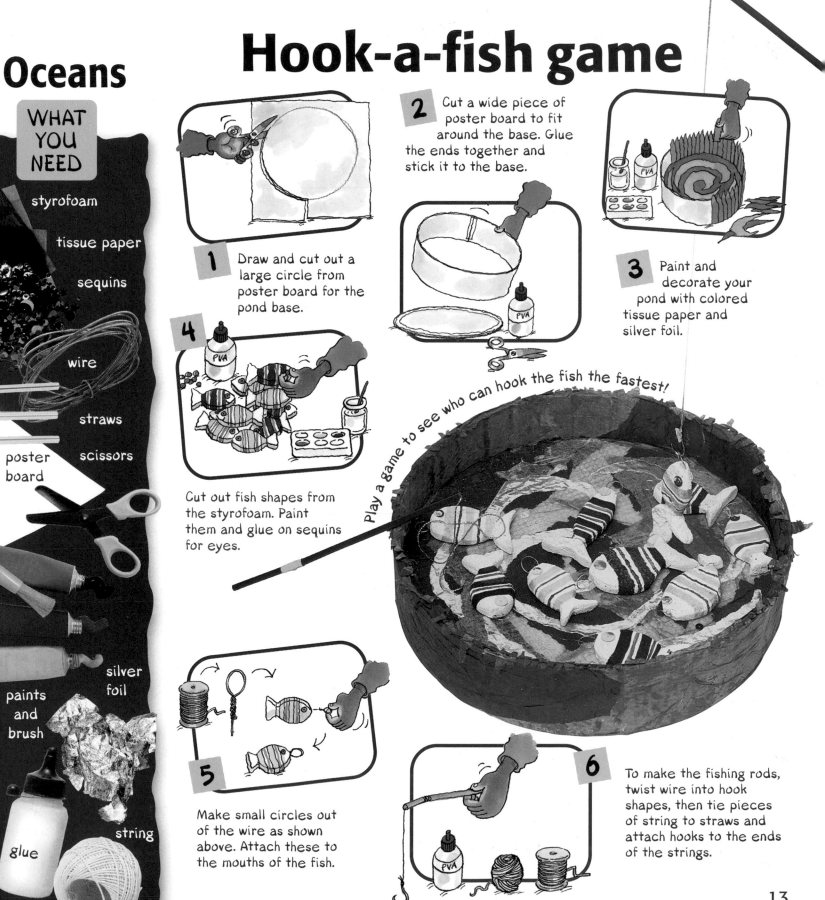

1 Draw and cut out a large circle from poster board for the pond base.

2 Cut a wide piece of poster board to fit around the base. Glue the ends together and stick it to the base.

3 Paint and decorate your pond with colored tissue paper and silver foil.

4 Cut out fish shapes from the styrofoam. Paint them and glue on sequins for eyes.

5 Make small circles out of the wire as shown above. Attach these to the mouths of the fish.

6 To make the fishing rods, twist wire into hook shapes, then tie pieces of string to straws and attach hooks to the ends of the strings.

Play a game to see who can hook the fish the fastest!

13

Sea cows

A manatee feeding its young.

Sea cows graze on sea grass, or seaweed, which is how they got their name. There are two types of sea cows, dugongs and manatees. Sea cows are mammals, which means they breathe air and give birth to live babies that feed on the mother's milk.

Home of the sea cow

Dugongs and manatees look very similar, but are slightly different and are found in different parts of the world. West Indian and West African manatees live in the tropical waters of the Atlantic Ocean. Amazonian manatees are smaller, and live in South America in the freshwater of the Amazon River. Dugongs are found in the Arabian Gulf, on Africa's east coast, in the Pacific Ocean, and in large numbers off northern Australia. The dugong has a dolphin-like tail and more rounded flippers than the manatee, which has a paddle-shaped tail.

Life underwater

Sea cows grow to about 10 feet (3 m) long and weigh around 1,100 pounds (500 kg). They live in warm, shallow waters and leave behind trails of bare sand and uprooted sea grass when they graze. Sea cows can stay underwater for 20 minutes before coming to the surface to breathe. They live to be about 50 years old.

Mermaids

Years ago, many sailors believed they had seen mermaids at sea. It is more likely that the sailors had seen a manatee or dugong, and mistaken it for a mermaid!

Oceans

Magical mermaid

WHAT YOU NEED

- sequins
- glitter
- scraps of material
- sand
- seaweed or yarn
- poster board
- shells
- scissors
- clay
- paints and brush
- pencil
- glue

1

Soften clay and make a mermaid's head and body with it. When dry, paint the body parts.

2 Draw the two sides of a mermaid's tail on material and cut out. Glue the sides together, leaving a gap at the top. Cut sequins into pieces, and glue onto the tail.

3

Fill the tail with sand and glue the hole closed. Then glue the body to the top of the tail.

Make other glittery accessories for your mermaid

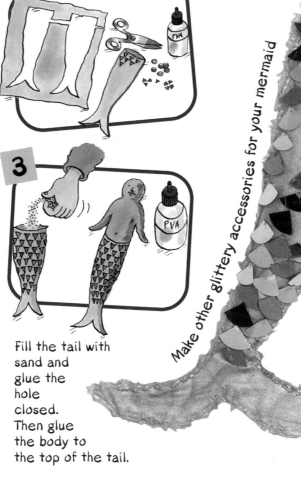

4 Glue a shell bikini top onto the mermaid's body. Glue seaweed or yarn on her head for hair.

5 Draw and cut out a comb and mirror from poster board. Decorate with sequins and glitter.

Ice fields

The North Pole is surrounded by the frozen Arctic Ocean, and the South Pole by the icy continent of **Antarctica**. The poles are the coldest and most remote places in the world, yet animals live there.

Polar bears

Polar bears have thick white coats to keep them warm and make them difficult to see in the white snowy landscape of the **Arctic**. When hunting for seals, a polar bear wanders alone over the floating ice sheets, called ice floes, looking for holes where seals come up for air. The polar bear waits patiently at the hole until a seal appears. Then, with one blow of the bear's paw and a bite at the back of the head, the seal is killed.

Seals

Seals are found at both poles. Some species spend the winter under the ice sheet, and can stay underwater for up to 70 minutes before coming up for air. Seals go on land to **breed** and give birth. Baby seals, called pups, are covered in white woolly fur, which they shed after one month.

Penguins

In the Antarctic, millions of penguins gather together in the summer to breed. Emperor penguins are the largest species of penguins and breed at the start of winter. The male emperor penguin keeps the newly laid egg warm by keeping it on his feet, off the cold ice. The male cannot eat during this time, and when the chick finally hatches, he has lost half his body weight. Penguins are not like most birds because they cannot fly. They have flippers instead of wings and move better in water than on land, swimming and diving so well that they have been mistaken for dolphins.

Emperor penguins on the Antarctic ice.

Oceans

Penguin family

1 Draw three different size penguins on cardboard. Paint and cut them out.

Create a chilly polar scene with stand-up penguin models!

2 Decorate a piece of poster board with paint, glitter, and tin foil to make an icy background.

3 Draw and cut out the shapes shown. Glue them to the backs of the penguins to make them stand up.

4 Stand the penguins up in front of the icy background.

Tidal pools

If you take a stroll along a beach you are bound to find a tidal pool. A variety of animals and plants, from starfish to seaweed, live together in a tidal pool. Plants and animals make their homes in these tiny sea worlds, where they help each other live.

High and low tides

Tidal pools change twice a day by the rise and fall of the **tides**. They fill up with salty seawater when the tide comes in, and then empty again when the tide goes out. Large, crushing waves and brisk ocean winds also affect the tidal pools. Seashore plants and animals have learned to **adapt** to life in an environment that changes all the time.

Different kinds of pools

Tidal pools can be small, shallow puddles high up on the shore, or large, deep holes close to the sea. When the tides come in, the seawater brings fresh oxygen and food for the tidal pool inhabitants.

Tidal pool neighbors

All kinds of ocean animals live together in a tidal pool. Velvet swimming crabs scurry on the rocks, the common starfish moves through the water in search of food, mollusks such as winkles, whelks, and limpets move slowly on their large fleshy feet. Tiny fish called blennies dart behind the water plants. Seaweed is essential to life in a tidal pool because it provides oxygen and shelter from the sun, and protects animals such as shrimp, crab, and fish from **predators**. Animals, such as slugs and snails, also eat these nutritious sea plants.

A red starfish

Oceans

3-D seashore picture

WHAT YOU NEED

glue

shoebox lid

shells and pebbles

feathers

cardboard

glitter

paints and brush

ruler

pencil

clay

sand

scissors

1 Make two cardboard rectangles to fit lengthwise inside the box lid. Make two rectangles that fit across the width of the box lid.

2 Cut slits in the two shorter pieces and slot all four pieces together. Place inside the lid.

3 Paint the lid and sections. Glue shells all around the outside.

4 Glue glitter and sand inside the sections.

5 Fill the spaces with shells, feathers, and pebbles, then glue them in.

Make starfish shapes from clay. When dry, paint and place in your treasure box

Oily feathers

The sea is a living world. There is an enormous variety of marine life beneath the waves, from sea plants and tiny **plankton** to huge whales and sharks. Today, **pollution** is threatening marine life and poisoning the fish that people eat.

Oil spills

The worst ocean polluter is oil. When oil tankers clean their tanks, they leave oil on the surface of the sea, which poisons fish and coats the feathers of sea birds. The oil clogs an animal's fur or a bird's feathers, and they can no longer swim or fly. They cannot keep warm and either die from cold, or poisoning caused by swallowing oil while trying to clean themselves. Rescue teams help by cleaning the birds and animals.

People pollute

Half of the world's population lives on or near the coasts and many people visit beaches on vacations. All this activity leads to a greater amount of garbage going into the sea. Litter kills ocean plants and animals. Plastic packaging can strangle or suffocate animals, and glass and metal can cut them. Farms and factories also produce chemicals which are washed into the sea.

Controlling pollution

Countries have to agree on laws to stop dumping waste into the sea, and to ban farms and factories from using pollutants. People can help by recycling their garbage and not leaving litter on beaches.

A sea bird covered in oil.

Oceans

Diving bird mobile

elastic

poster board

paints and brush

glue

tin foil

gold thread

needle

scissors

pencil

black and brown pastels

1 On poster board, draw the outline of a diving bird and its wings. Cut them out.

2 Cover the underside of the wings with tin foil.

3 Color the rest of your bird with dark brown and black pastels and paints.

4 Make a fold along the inside edge of each wing and glue the wings onto the body of the bird.

5 Attach a piece of gold thread from the top of the body and elastic from each wing. Knot them together.

Push the wings gently and see how they move up and down.

Make other bird mobiles to fly in the breeze with your diving bird

Sea salt

Some of the salt we use in our food comes from the sea. Salt is important to us because we need salt to stay healthy and replace the salt our bodies lose when we sweat. Most of the salt we use comes from rock salt mines, but many people get their salt from the sea.

Salt pans

The sea contains a large amount of salt. In dry, hot countries, such as India and Africa, shallow pools, called pans, are built on the seashore. Sea water is pumped into these pans, then left to dry out, leaving the powdery salt behind.

The Dead Sea

The saltiest water in the world is in the Dead Sea, on the border of Jordan and Israel. It is called dead because only brine shrimp and some plants can live in it. The Dead Sea is about 50 miles (80 km) long, and its shore is the lowest place on Earth, at about 1,300 feet (399 m) below sea level.

Flamingos in Florida

Flamingos are birds that can stand high levels of salt. During the hurricane season, the shores of Florida flood. As the water evaporates, it turns salty and brine shrimp hatch. Flamingos feed the shrimp to their hungry **fledglings**.

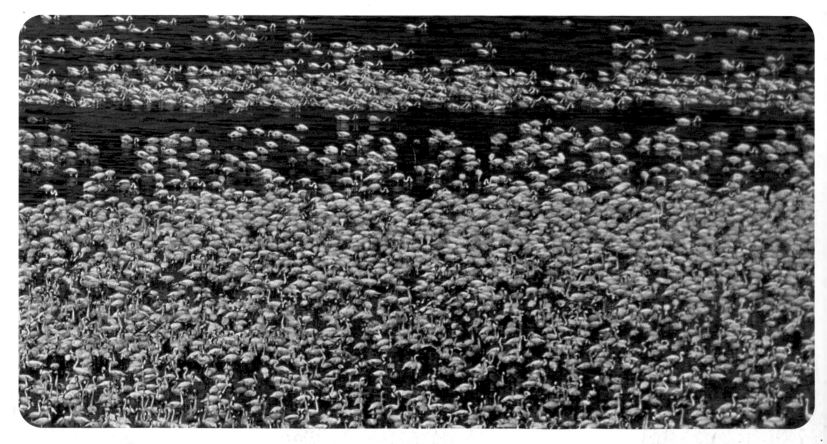

Salt dough flamingo

WHAT
YOU
NEED

bowl

glitter

oil

salt

flour

water

paints and brush

wooden spoon

1 Mix salt, oil, flour, and water together in a bowl until you have a doughy mixture. Place the dough in the fridge for a few hours.

2 Flatten some of the dough into a circle for a background. Make a landscape and flamingo with the rest of the dough and place them on top.

3 Bake at 375°F (190°C) for 30 minutes. When cool, paint and decorate with glitter. Remember to ask an adult to help you!

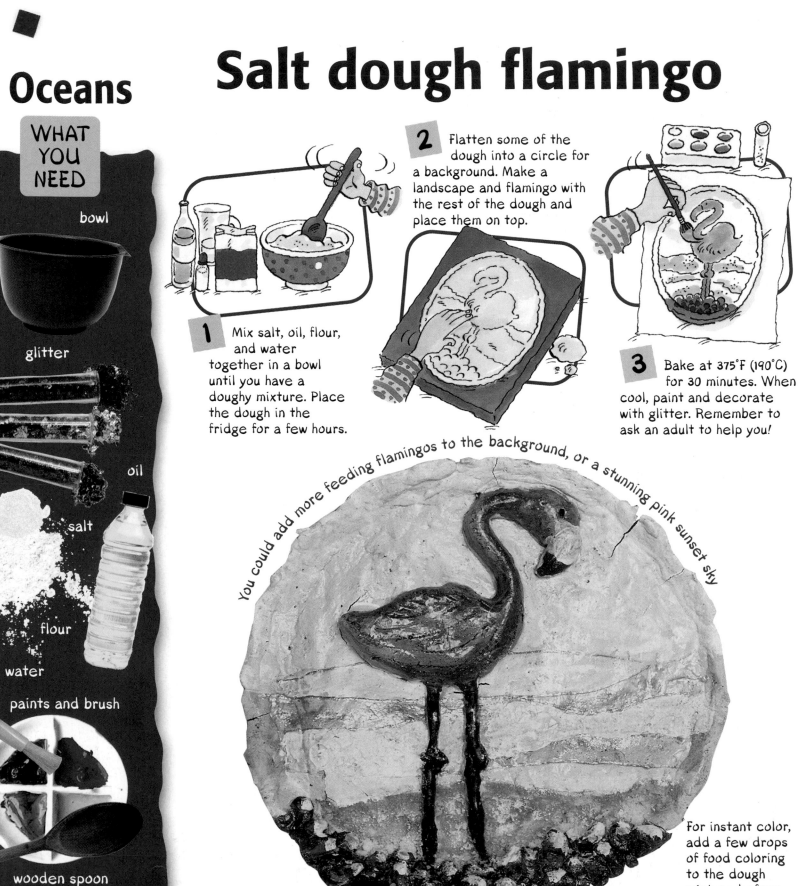

You could add more feeding flamingos to the background, or a stunning pink sunset sky

For instant color, add a few drops of food coloring to the dough mixture before you bake it.

23

Turtle tale

Thousands of years ago, turtles left the land to live in the sea. Over time, turtles adapted to life in the salty ocean by developing flippers instead of legs, and crying salty tears to get rid of the salt they absorbed from the sea. Turtles still come to the surface for air, and females come ashore to lay eggs.

Laying eggs

After **mating** at sea, female turtles go ashore at night. They always return to the same beach where they themselves hatched, even if they have to travel thousands of miles across the ocean. On the beach, the mother turtle digs a deep hole where she lays a **clutch** of up to 200 eggs, each egg about the size of a table tennis ball. She covers the eggs with sand, then returns to the sea. A female turtle may only breed once every three years but may come ashore several times in one season to lay her eggs.

Up and away

The eggs stay buried for several weeks. Eventually, the babies hatch and start to dig their way out. Baby turtles know if it is day or night by the temperature of the sand, and only come out at night when there are fewer predators around. If the sand near the surface is hot, it is daytime, but when the sand is cool they know it is nighttime and they make their way out and head for the sea.

A difficult journey

As the little turtles head for the sea, sea birds, crabs, iguanas, and even foxes are waiting to hunt them. Many baby turtles that survive the dangerous journey to the sea will be eaten by fish. Turtles that live to be adults are threatened by people, who hunt turtles for their shells and meat.

The loggerhead turtle was given its name because of its large head.

Oceans

Loggerhead turtle

1 Blow up the balloon and paste several layers of newspaper strips all over with watered-down glue. Leave to dry and then burst the balloon.

2 Mix paint with glue and cover the newspaper shell with swirly circles.

3 Soften the clay by rolling it in your hands and make the head, feet, and flippers of your turtle. Leave to dry and then paint them.

Create a turtle family with multi-colored shells and flippers

4 Cut around the shell as shown.

5 Fill the nylons with newspaper and use to stuff the shell.

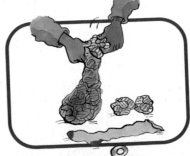

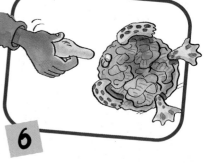

6 Make holes in the nylons and glue in the head, feet, and flippers.

On stilts

On tropical coasts, where forests come down to the water's edge, you will find tall trees known as **mangroves** standing on a thick tangle of roots. Here, the tide washes in and out and the plants have adapted to living in salty water.

Surviving salt

Most trees cannot grow in waterlogged ground because the soil is too soft to support them and it lacks the oxygen tree roots need. Trees in mangrove swamps live in thick mud, starved of oxygen, with their roots pickled in salt water. Mangroves survive because of their two special types of roots. Stilt roots arch out from the trunk to support the tree, and breathing roots push up above the mud to take in oxygen. Mangrove trees are also able to get rid of salt through small holes, called glands, in their leaves.

Life in the mangroves

Many birds and animals live in mangrove swamps. Mangrove tree crabs live in the branches of the trees, only dropping into the water to escape danger. The mangrove cuckoo feeds on swamp insects, while several types of sea snails munch mangrove leaves. The mudskipper is a fish that can breathe in both water and air. It has strong fins that help it move across the mud. The Malayan mudskipper has fins that form suckers under its body so it can cling to wet trees.

Mangrove trees rising from the swamp.

Oceans

Make a roots and branches picture of mangrove trees

WHAT YOU NEED

- pencil
- pencil crayons
- tissue paper
- glue
- paints and brush
- scissors
- poster board
- gold paper
- wire
- glitter
- clear acetate

1 On poster board draw two mangrove trees with their branches above sea level and their roots below, as shown. Add a forest background.

Paint and decorate with glitter and colored pencils.

2

3 Cover the watery half of your picture with clear acetate.

4 Make a third tree by twisting strands of wire together to form the trunk, branches, and roots. Attach the wire tree to the center of your picture by pushing wire strands through the poster board and fastening them at the back.

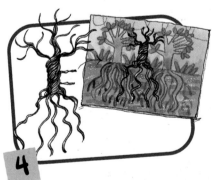

5 Cut leaves from tissue paper and gold paper and stick to the wire frame. Mount your picture.

27

Desert islands

The ocean floor has all the features we see on land, such as mountains, valleys, and volcanoes, but they lie in the depths of the sea, so we cannot see them. Sometimes the peaks of these underwater mountains or volcanoes poke up through the waves. They form small islands, either on their own or in groups or chains. Islands are scattered throughout the world's oceans.

The Galapagos Islands

All islands are separate from the **mainland**. Rare species of plants and animals are often found on islands, where they are safe from mainland predators. The Galapagos Islands in the Pacific Ocean are named after the giant tortoises that live there – "galapagos" means "tortoise." They live for up to 200 years, and the males weigh as much as 550 pounds (250 kg).

A marine iguana from the Galapagos Islands.

Other rare Galapagos animals include the marine iguana, which is the only lizard to live and feed in the sea, and the flightless cormorant, a large bird that does not fly.

Pirates

Islands have always been good hiding places for pirates because they can ambush, or make a surprise attack on, passing ships. In the 17th and 18th centuries, pirates known as buccaneers prowled along the coasts of America. The buccaneers were waiting to attack the great Spanish **galleons** loaded with treasure that were sailing home to Spain across the Atlantic Ocean. In the 18th century, when Dutch and British ships traded with China and Japan, they had to pass through the Straits of Malacca, between Malaysia and Sumatra. There, pirates would wait on the islands and attack passing ships. Today, piracy is still a danger in some parts of the world.

Coral islands

Coral islands, like the Maldives, lie in the warm waters of the Indian and Pacific Oceans. These islands form when soil and vegetation settle on coral atolls. A coral atoll is a ring of coral layers that has built up on a sunken mudbank or on the rim of the crater of a sunken volcano. Seeds brought by the wind or sea, such as coconuts, grow on the shores.

Treasure island

WHAT YOU NEED

paper

pencil

paints and brush

black pen

tea bags

water

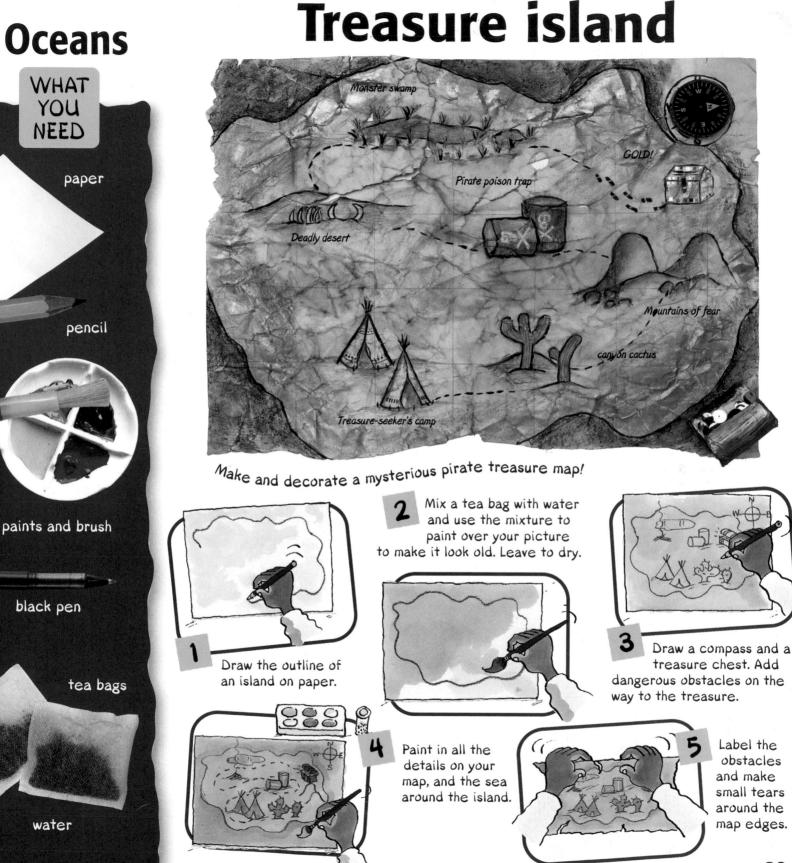

Monster swamp

GOLD!

Pirate poison trap

Deadly desert

Mountains of fear

canyon cactus

Treasure-seeker's camp

Make and decorate a mysterious pirate treasure map!

1 Draw the outline of an island on paper.

2 Mix a tea bag with water and use the mixture to paint over your picture to make it look old. Leave to dry.

3 Draw a compass and a treasure chest. Add dangerous obstacles on the way to the treasure.

4 Paint in all the details on your map, and the sea around the island.

5 Label the obstacles and make small tears around the map edges.

29

Deep-sea fish

Many strange and wonderful fish live in the deepest part of the ocean. This area is called the **bathypelagic zone**. It stretches from 3,300 to 13,000 feet (1 to 6 km) below the water's surface. From 2 miles (3 km) down there is almost no light.

Bioluminescence

The hatchet fish and the black devil deep-sea angler are two fish that can make their own light by a process called bioluminescence. A chemical in the fish changes the energy stored in the fish's cells into light. The fish uses this light to search for food or to attract prey.

Useful eyes

The eyes of some deep-sea fish are attached to short stalks protruding from their head. The eyes can turn in many directions, so the fish can look up, as well as to the front and side.

Strange shapes

Some deep-sea fish have strange shapes. The common gulper eel looks like a long tail with a mouth attached. The tripod, or spider fish, looks like a three-legged stool with its three long fins, which it uses to sit on the ocean floor. The Pacific fangtooth has a large mouth with rows of long, curved, needle-sharp teeth.

30

Oceans

Fishy monster

WHAT YOU NEED

- colored paper
- pencil
- old sock
- two bottle caps
- glue
- scissors
- newspaper
- sand
- paints and brush

1 Stuff the sock with scrunched-up strips of newspaper. Glue or tie the end of the sock closed.

2 To make the upper fin, fold a piece of paper the same length of your fish. Mark out a zig-zag shape and cut it out.

3 Glue the zig-zag fin to the fish.

Make a weird creature from the deep!

4 To make the tail and side fins, fold the colored paper like a fan and cut it into three pieces, one big and two small pieces. Glue on the big piece for the tail fin and the two small pieces for the side fins.

5 Mix the sand, glue, and paint together and brush the mixture over the fish shape. Leave to dry. Glue on the bottle caps for the eyes.

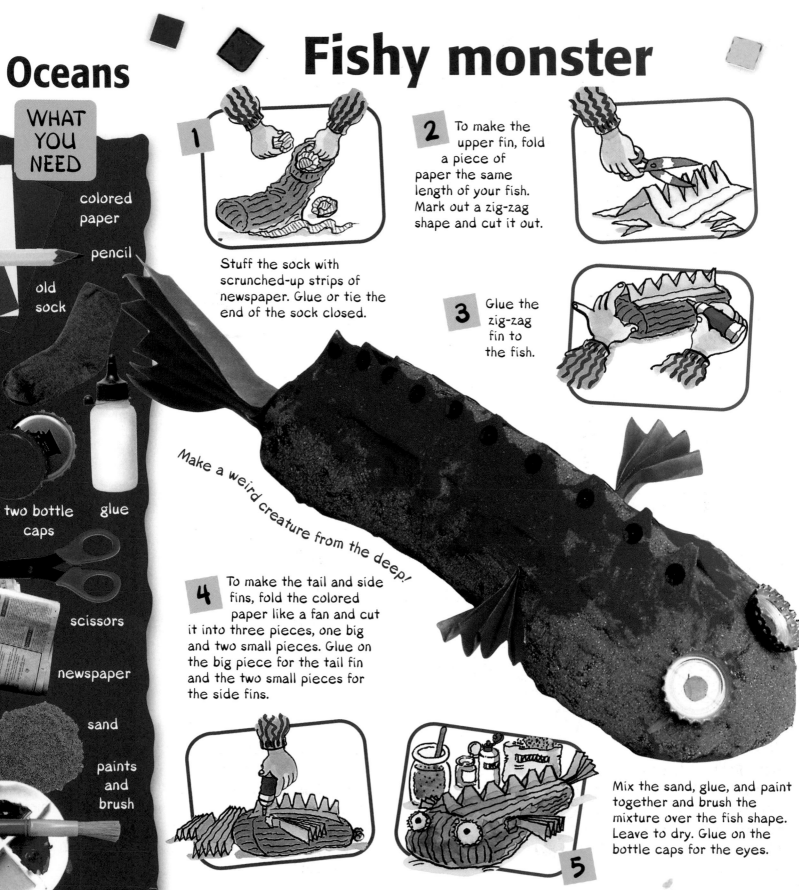

High tide, low tide

Exploring the beach is fun, but it can also be dangerous! Waves can rush up the beach and cut you off from the shore. When the sea rises, it is called high tide. After approximately six hours, the sea begins to sink. When the sea goes out, or moves away from shore, it is low tide.

The pull of gravity

When Earth spins, the force called **gravity** stops everything from flying off it. Gravity pulls the Moon toward the Earth. The Moon has its own gravity, which is strong enough to pull on the sea nearest to it, as it goes around Earth. This pull causes tides, which in most parts of the world change every six hours.

Spring and neap tides

The Sun also has a pulling effect on the sea. Twice a month both the Sun and the Moon pull together, causing very high and very low tides known as spring tides. Twice a month the pull of the Sun and Moon is not strong, causing smaller tides called neap tides. The highest tide in the world takes place in the Bay of Fundy, in Nova Scotia, Canada, where it can rise 52 feet (16 m), or as high as a four-story building.

Waves and currents

When the wind blows on the surface of the sea, it makes waves. Strong winds can also cause currents, which are like rivers of cold and warm water that travel around the oceans. Currents on the surface of the sea, such as Florida's Gulf Stream, are driven by the wind. Deep ocean currents come from the cold **polar regions** and flow beneath the warmer water.

Oceans

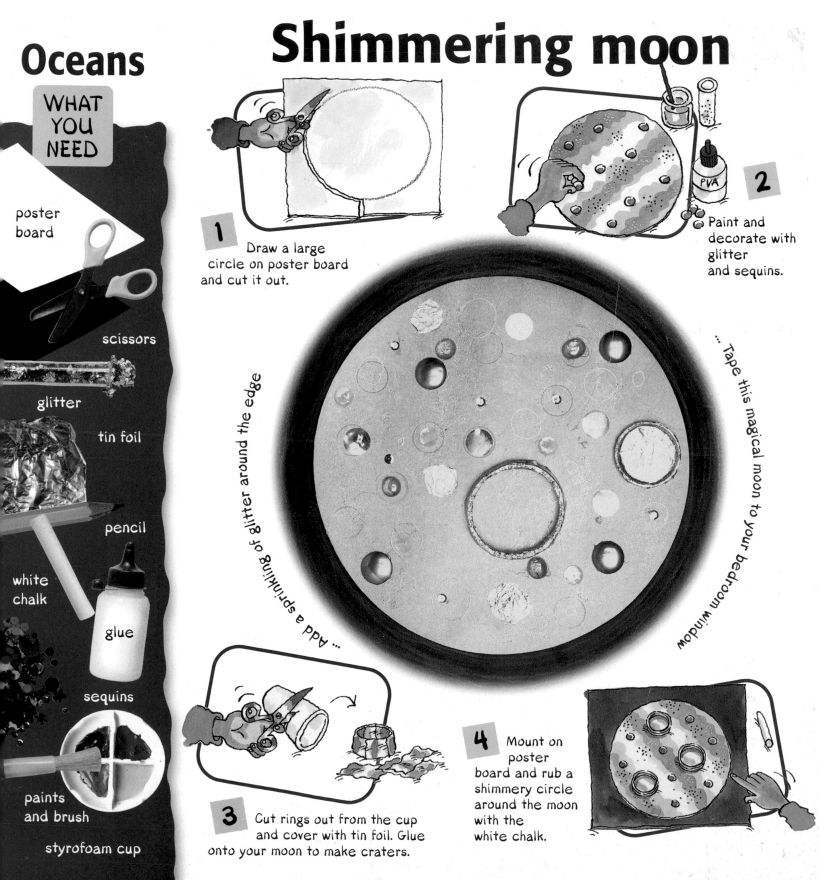

WHAT YOU NEED

- poster board
- scissors
- glitter
- tin foil
- pencil
- white chalk
- glue
- sequins
- paints and brush
- styrofoam cup

1 Draw a large circle on poster board and cut it out.

2 Paint and decorate with glitter and sequins.

... Add a sprinkling of glitter around the edge

... Tape this magical moon to your bedroom window

3 Cut rings out from the cup and cover with tin foil. Glue onto your moon to make craters.

4 Mount on poster board and rub a shimmery circle around the moon with the white chalk.

33

Legs and suckers

What sea animal can change color, has eight legs with suckers on them, can squirt out a black fluid called **ink**, has eyes similar to a human's and is considered to be the most intelligent of the invertebrates? An octopus, of course!

Suckers

An octopus may have as many as 240 suckers on its eight tentacles, or arms. Once an octopus has attached itself to something, there is no escape! If the octopus loses one of its tentacles, another one grows back.

Living alone

There are about 200 different types of octopuses. They are found inside caves in shallow seas near the shore. Octopuses live alone.

A brainy animal

The octopus is considered the most intelligent of the invertebrates. Experiments show that an octopus can remove the lid from a jar and get the food from inside. Octopus eyes are more like human eyes than any other invertebrate's because they are able to see images.

Defending itself

An octopus does not have a shell, so it protects itself from predators in other ways. The octopus is a master of disguise. It changes color to match its surroundings. If threatened, an octopus will release a cloud of black ink to temporarily blind its enemy and destroy its sense of smell.

An octopus swimming in the sea.

Oceans

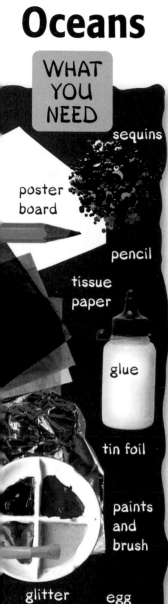

WHAT YOU NEED

sequins

poster board

pencil

tissue paper

glue

tin foil

paints and brush

glitter

egg carton

scissors

four pairs of nylons

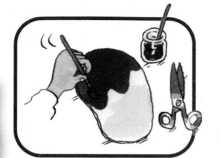

1 Draw an octopus head on poster board. Cut out and paint the head.

4 Stuff all four pairs of nylons with scrunched up tissue paper. Glue to the back of the octopus to make eight tentacles.

5 Glue blue tissue paper on a sheet of poster board. Glue on scrunched up tissue paper rocks.

Glue the octopus in place. Make eyes from tin foil and sequins. Glue sequins on the tentacles.

2 Cut out individual segments from the egg carton and paint.

3 Glue the egg carton segments onto the octopus's body and decorate them with sequins.

Cut out and paint fish and starfish shapes and glue them to your picture. Decorate with glitter.

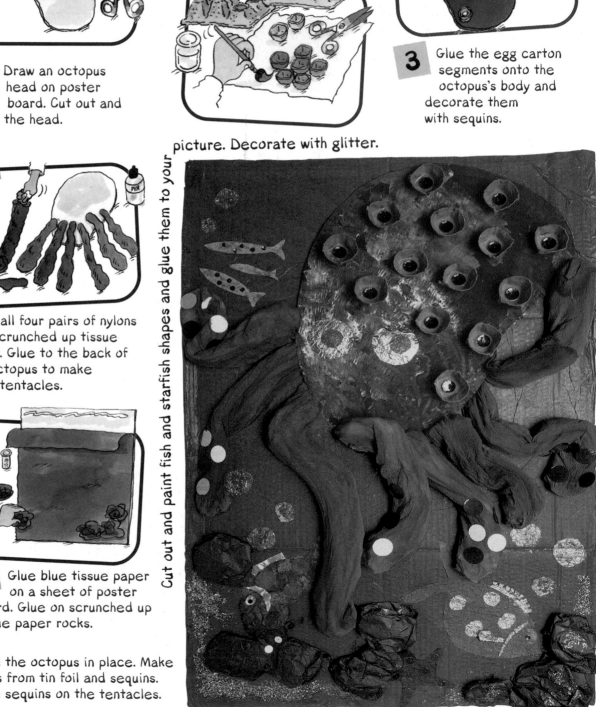

Ocean giants

Most whales are enormous animals, but they move gracefully through their watery world, swimming, diving, rolling, and leaping. They come up to the surface and breathe out a great spray, and immediately take in more air. Then, with an upward thrust of their large tail fins, they dive back down into the deep waters in search of food.

What is a whale?

A whale is not a fish. It is a mammal like us, which means it is warm-blooded and gives birth to babies that feed on their mother's milk. A whale breathes air, but its nostrils, called a **blowhole**, are on the top of its head!

Ocean giants

The blue whale is the biggest animal that has ever existed. At 165 tons (150 tonnes), it is as heavy as about 25 elephants and can grow to more than 98 feet (30 m) long. Blue whales have the biggest babies in the world, weighing 1,000 times more than a human baby at birth! The baby whale eats krill, swallowing hundreds in one gulp.

Whales in danger

Over the centuries, whales have been hunted for their blubber, or fat, meat, and baleen – a comb-like plate in some whales' mouths that they use to filter food from the water. The number of whales in the oceans has been greatly reduced by hunting, and some species of whale have almost died out. There is now a worldwide ban on killing whales for money.

Oceans

Paper mâché whale

WHAT YOU NEED

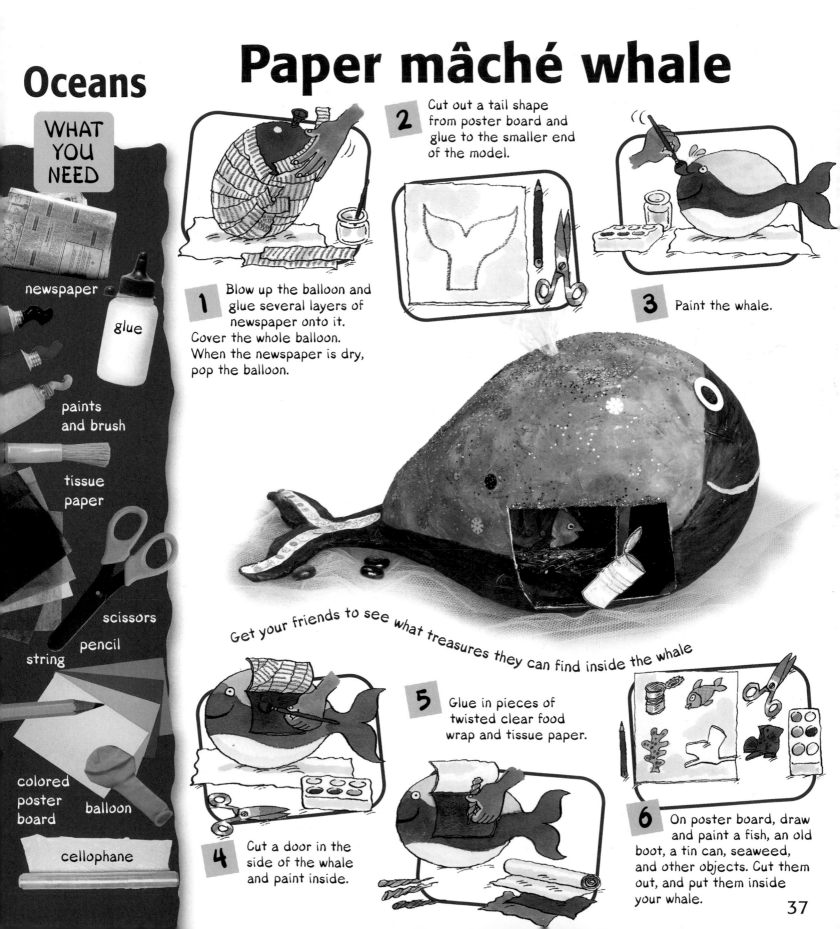

newspaper

glue

paints and brush

tissue paper

scissors

pencil

string

colored poster board

balloon

cellophane

1 Blow up the balloon and glue several layers of newspaper onto it. Cover the whole balloon. When the newspaper is dry, pop the balloon.

2 Cut out a tail shape from poster board and glue to the smaller end of the model.

3 Paint the whale.

Get your friends to see what treasures they can find inside the whale

4 Cut a door in the side of the whale and paint inside.

5 Glue in pieces of twisted clear food wrap and tissue paper.

6 On poster board, draw and paint a fish, an old boot, a tin can, seaweed, and other objects. Cut them out, and put them inside your whale.

37

Jewels of the sea

Diatoms magnified many times.

The top layer of the ocean is warmer than the water below it. It receives plenty of sunlight and is the perfect place for microscopic plants, called **plankton**, to grow. These plants use sunlight to make their own food, in a process called **photosynthesis**. **Diatoms** are a type of plankton. They are found in every ocean, just below the surface. There are hundreds of diatoms in one drop of water.

Shimmering cases

There are several thousand types of diatoms in all different shapes and sizes. Some join together in patterns, and others float on their own like tiny, glistening gems. Diatoms look like blobs of jelly inside a hard glassy shell. This shell, or case, is made of **silica**. Some diatoms contain tiny drops of oil that help them float in water. When a diatom dies, its silica case drops down to the ocean floor.

Sea food

Plankton is not just made up of plants. Tiny animals, called zooplankton, are also part of it. Plant plankton, including diatoms, is called phytoplankton. Phytoplankton is the first part of the ocean **food chain**, providing food for the zooplankton, which is then eaten by small fish. Larger fish then eat the small fish.

Skeleton power

Toothpaste and scouring powder contain the remains of tiny **fossilized** diatoms. Over millions of years, the silica skeletons have been pressed down until the bottom layer becomes fossilized, or turned to stone. The strength of the silica makes it suitable to use for grinding, sanding, smoothing, or polishing.

Oceans

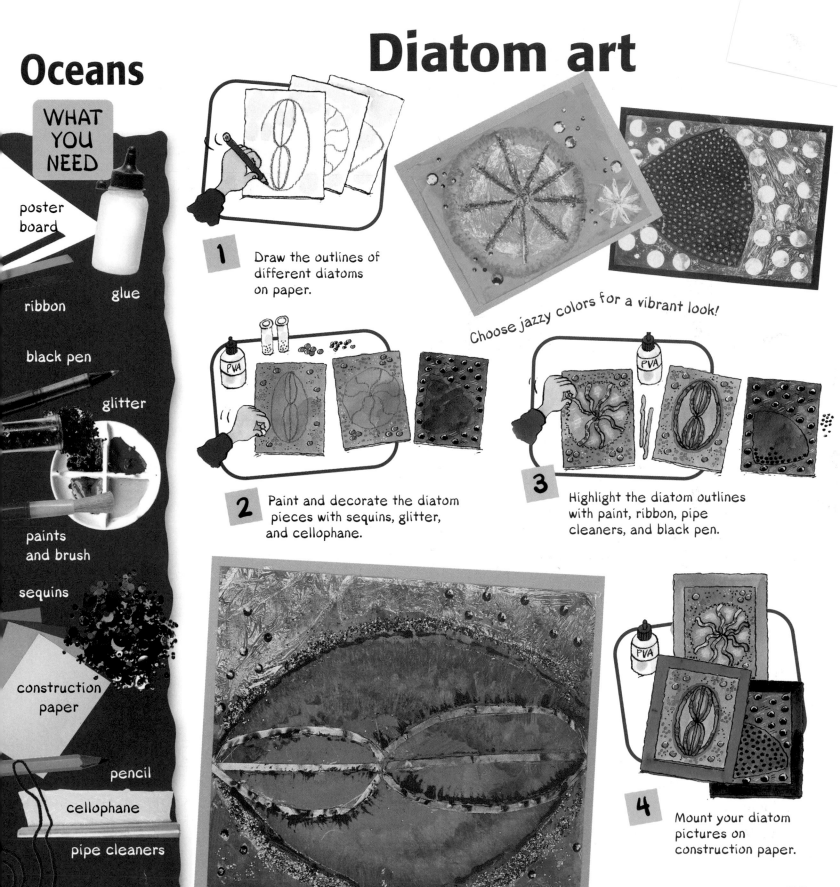

WHAT YOU NEED

poster board

ribbon

glue

black pen

glitter

paints and brush

sequins

construction paper

pencil

cellophane

pipe cleaners

Diatom art

1 Draw the outlines of different diatoms on paper.

Choose jazzy colors for a vibrant look!

2 Paint and decorate the diatom pieces with sequins, glitter, and cellophane.

3 Highlight the diatom outlines with paint, ribbon, pipe cleaners, and black pen.

4 Mount your diatom pictures on construction paper.

39

Seahorses

The seahorse is a small fish, although it does not look like one. Its head looks like a tiny horse head, and that is where it gets its name. It has a body made up of bony plates, a long snout and cylindrical-shaped mouth, and a long flexible tail to grasp on to sea plants. There are 35 different types of seahorse, from the tiny dwarf seahorse, which is only one inch (2.5 cm) long, to one that is about 12 inches (30 cm) long.

Lifestyle

Seahorses are found in warm seas near the shoreline, and hidden among the seaweed, clinging to it with their tails. They are not very fast swimmers, so they have to rely on camouflage to keep safe. There are plenty of crab, tuna, and rays around to hunt them. Some seahorses can change color to blend in with their surroundings. Others grow leafy fronds to make them look like seaweed. Their seaweed appearance makes seahorses hard to spot.

Male seahorses

Seahorses have the same mate throughout their lives, but it is the male seahorse that gives birth to the babies. During their mating dance, male and female seahorses twirl around, raise their heads, and even turn fluorescent colors! The female seahorse lays hundreds of eggs into a pouch on the front of the male's body. After about three weeks the baby seahorses are born. Baby seahorses are fed, given oxygen, and kept safe in the father's pouch. Baby seahorses face many dangers, such as storms that tear them from their parents and leave them to starve. These dangers mean only two of every hundred seahorses live to adulthood.

A colorful pygmy seahorse.

Oceans

Watery grotto

WHAT YOU NEED

paints and brush

colored paper

poster board

scissors

pencil

tissue paper

ribbon

tin foil

glue

sponge

cellophane

1 Tear strips of tissue paper and glue onto poster board.

2 Draw outlines of fish, crab, and starfish on another piece of poster board. Paint and cut out. Glue to your tissue paper background.

Glue on pieces of cellophane for a watery effect

3 Make coral shapes from colored paper and sponges. Paint and glue onto the sea scene.

4 Make seaweed by gluing strands of tin foil, ribbon, and tissue paper onto the picture.

5 Draw outlines of seahorses on dark paper, cut out the silhouettes and glue onto the picture.

Down, down, down

What lies beneath the ocean waves? People have always wondered what mysteries lie in the ocean's dark depths. Many different methods of exploring oceans have been tried over the centuries. Divers are continually discovering more of the secrets of the world's oceans.

Sponge diving

The earliest form of diving involved divers simply holding their breath for a long time underwater. Early sponge divers in the Mediterranean dove off a boat to depths of 98 feet (30 m).

When they ran out of breath, divers had to come back to the surface. In the mid-nineteenth century, divers started wearing heavy diving suits with an air supply connected to the helmet. This allowed them to go to a depth of 230 feet (70 m). Diving this deep created a new problem called "the bends." Divers sometimes experienced dizziness, breathing problems, and pain when they returned to the surface. If divers came back up to the surface too quickly, the **nitrogen** in their air supply formed bubbles in their blood and this often lead to death. Divers had to find a new way of dealing with "the bends." Today, sponge divers wear lightweight suits and breathe filtered air.

What is scuba?

SCUBA stands for Self-Contained Underwater Breathing Apparatus. Scuba equipment was invented in 1943 by Jacques Cousteau and Emile Gagnan. Divers breathe air from oxygen tanks fitted onto their backs. This lets them move around freely while they are underwater. Scientists scuba-dive to study the oceans, marine life, and to **salvage** wrecks. Many people scuba-dive for enjoyment, to explore reefs, and to take underwater pictures.

Oceans

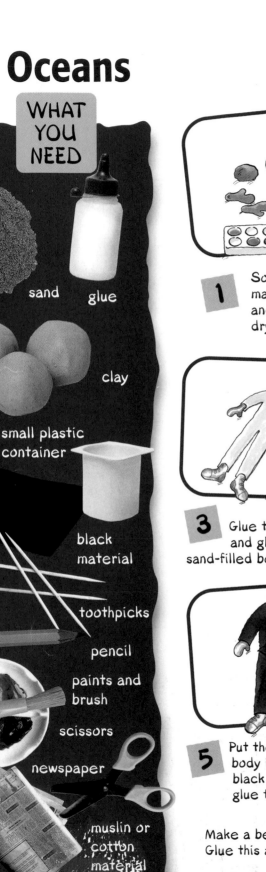

WHAT YOU NEED

sand

glue

clay

small plastic container

black material

toothpicks

pencil

paints and brush

scissors

newspaper

muslin or cotton material

1 Soften the clay and make a head, boots, and gloves. Leave to dry, then paint.

3 Glue the head, boots, and gloves onto the sand-filled body.

5 Put the muslin body into the black suit and glue together.

Make a belt from a strip of paper. Glue this around your diver.

2 Cut two body shapes out of the muslin and glue together, leaving a hole at the top. Fill the body with sand, then glue the hole shut.

4 Draw two bigger body outlines on the black material. Cut out and cover both with PVA glue to make the material stiff. Leave to dry.

6 Cut the plastic container into a helmet shape. Glue on strips of newspaper. Leave to dry and paint. Make a grid from toothpicks to fit across the front of the helmet.

Watery graves

The world's ocean beds are turning into underwater junkyards, scattered with the remains of wrecked ships. Shipwrecks from long ago tell a story and are a kind of time capsule. The remains can tell us how ships were built and how the people from a particular time in history lived. Shipwrecks might also hold amazing hidden treasures, such as coins or jewels from long ago.

Wrecks

Shipwrecks are usually caused by a ship hitting rocks. The collision can happen because somebody makes a mistake, a sea chart is wrong, or an engine fails. A ship may collide with another in a fog, or with an **iceberg** as the *Titanic* did. Other ships may have encountered a storm at sea, or been attacked by enemy ships at war, like the *Mary Rose*.

Past and present

The *Mary Rose*, an English warship, sank in 1545 and was found by accident. In 1836, a fishing boat's nets got caught on the seabed near the coastal town of Portsmouth, England. By coincidence some divers were exploring a nearby wreck, a wooden warship, the *Royal George*, that had sunk in 1782. They also recovered bronze cannon and iron guns from the *Mary Rose*, but it was only in the 1970s that modern technology enabled the wreck and its treasures to be brought to land. Before the ship was brought to shore, divers took photographs of the ship and listed the 17,000 objects found on the sunken ship.

Oceans

WHAT YOU NEED

cardboard boxes

small pebbles

poster board

sand

egg cartons

colored construction paper

pencil

glue

sequins

tissue paper

paints and brush

scissors

Shipwreck!

2 Glue together boxes, cartons, and paper to form a ship. Cut out jagged edges for a hole in the ship. Paint the ship.

1 Spread glue over a piece of poster board and cover with sand.

3 Cover half of the base with blue tissue paper to form the sea. Use scrunched up paper and egg carton cups for rocks and paint.

4 Make a treasure chest from a small carton. Add sequins for treasure.

What other objects might have washed up on shore?

5 Glue the shipwreck and treasure chest onto the sand and sea base.

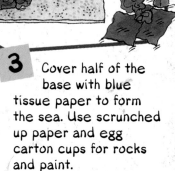

Glossary

absorb To take in another substance, such as a sponge taking in water.

adapt Changing over a long period of time to suit an environment.

Antarctica A large area of land around the South Pole that is completely covered with ice. Antarctica is one of the seven continents.

Arctic The region around the North Pole.

bacteria Tiny, one-celled organisms.

breed To produce offspring, or babies.

brine Another word for salt.

calcium A mineral that is found in animal teeth and bones.

camouflage A disguise used to hide from predators or prey in which a plant or animal looks like its surroundings.

cell The smallest and most basic parts of plants and animals.

chlorine A smelly gas.

clutch The complete number of eggs laid by a bird at one time.

coral A hard material made up of small sea animals called polyps.

crustacean An animal such as a crab or a shrimp with a hard outer shell that lives in water.

current A body of flowing water or air that moves in a specific direction.

dense Having parts tightly packed together.

diatom A tiny living form which is found in plankton.

endangered To be in danger of extinction.

fledgling A young bird.

food chain A series of plants and animals in which each is a source of food for the next in the series.

fossil The remains of a plant or animal, preserved in rock.

frond A feather-like piece of seaweed.

galleon A large sailing ship used mostly by the Spanish in the 15th to 17th centuries as warships or merchant ships.

gravity A natural force that causes small objects to move toward the Earth's center.

harpoon A spear attached to a rope, used for hunting whales and other large fish.

ice floe A piece of ice that has broken away from the main ice shelf.

iceberg A floating piece of ice in the sea. Part of the iceberg stands above the water, but most of it is below the surface of the water.

ink The dark liquid given off by an octopus in self-defense.

jet propulsion A way of moving through the water in which water or air is forced out the back of an object, causing the object to move in the opposite direction.

kelp A type of seaweed.

krill Tiny, shrimp-like crustaceans that form part of plankton.

mainland The main landmass of a country or continent.

mangrove Trees that live in salty water.

mate The male or female of a pair that come together to breed.

microscope An instrument for making objects appear larger.

mollusk A group of animals that have soft bodies. Some, such as snails, have a shell. Others, such as octopuses, do not.

nitrogen A colorless, odorless gas found in the atmosphere.

nutrient Nutrients are the good things found in food that help animals and plants live and grow.

overfishing Taking more fish from the sea that can be replaced by natural breeding.

photosynthesis The way in which plants use sunlight to make food.

plankton Microscopic plants and animals that float in the sea. Fish and whales eat plankton.

polar regions The areas around the North and South Poles.

pollution Pollution is caused by harmful chemicals or waste products which contaminate the environment.

predator An animal that hunts other animals for food.

prey An animal that is hunted by other animals for food.

salt White crystals, usually from the sea and used to flavor food.

salvage To rescue a ship or its cargo from the sea.

silica A white or colorless crystal compound used to make glass and concrete.

sponge A water animal that has a soft skeleton with many tiny holes.

tentacle A long, flexible extension on an animal used for feeling and grasping.

tide The rise and fall of the sea level caused by the gravitational pull of the Moon and the Sun on Earth.

tropics The warm areas of Earth close to the equator.

Index

Materials guide

WHAT YOU NEED

gold foil

silver foil

filler paste

PVA glue

flour

salt

cellophane or acetate

The crafts in this book require the use of materials and products that are easily purchased in craft stores. If you cannot locate some materials, you can substitute other materials with those we have listed here, or use your imagination to make the craft with what you have on hand.

Gold foil: can be found in craft stores. It is very delicate and sometimes tears.

Silver foil: can be found in craft stores. It is very delicate, soft and sometimes tears. For some crafts, tin or aluminum foil can be substituted. Aluminum foil is a less delicate material and makes a harder finished craft.

PVA glue: commonly called polyvinyl acetate. It is a modeling glue that creates a type of varnish when mixed with water. It is also used as a strong glue. In some crafts, other strong glues can be substituted, and used as an adhesive, but not as a varnish.

Filler paste: sometimes called plaster of Paris. It is a paste that hardens when it dries. It can be purchased at craft and hardware stores.

Paste: a paste of 1/2 cup flour, one tablespoon of salt and one cup of warm water can be made to paste strips of newspaper as in a papier mâché craft. Alternatively, wallpaper paste can be purchased and mixed as per directions on the package.

Cellophane: a clear or colored plastic material. Acetate can also be used in crafts that call for this material. Acetate is a clear, or colored, thin plastic that can be found in craft stores.

 1 2 3 4 5 6 7 8 9 0   Printed in the USA   0 9 8 7 6 5 4 3 2